Richard Branson: The Virgin Rebel Billionaire

Michael Joshua

DEDICATION

I would like to dedicate this book to all the wealth seekers and entrepreneurs out there. May you always have inspiration to not listen to the haters and to follow your dream. If Richard Branson could do it, so can you!

CONTENTS

THE PURPOSE OF THIS BOOK

The purpose of this book is to give you some insight into Richard Branson as a person, student, philanthropist, husband, entrepreneur and billionaire. By examining statements he's been quoted as saying, you will gain an understanding of Branson's ideology.

This book is not intended to be biased in any way. Although there isn't much to dislike about the guy, Branson's statements will be presented as light comments coming from a brilliant man who went for it all and made it work, even if it meant losing money. He lives on the edge, takes chances and is adored by many.

The intention of this book is to present a candid depiction of Richard Branson based upon what he has said and show you why this rebel billionaire of the Virgin enterprise has become a fascinating person to read about and learn from.

CHAPTER 1: STUDENT

Richard Branson, whose full name is Sir Richard Charles Nicholas Branson, wears many hats throughout his usual day. However, the man under the hat is one of a kind – a success story that continues to be in the making with each passing year.

The London-native is best known for being the founder of Virgin Group, the umbrella company that shields some 400 individual companies.

You could probably say that Branson got started when he was just sixteen years old. His first venture into business was *Student*, a magazine. By 1970, the young entrepreneur was already expanding his empire.

This very same year Branson opened a mail-order record business. Two years after this, the entrepreneur opened a chain of record stores. Originally, these stores were called Virgin Records, but they later became known as Virgin Megastores.

This Virgin brand Branson built grew rapidly, well into the 1980s. During this time, Branson set up the acclaimed Virgin Atlantic then expanded the music label Virgin Records.

Branson has constantly defeated the odds against him. The business mogul has dyslexia and performed poorly academically. If these two things aren't impressive enough to think about, you have to look at how Branson has turned lemons into lemonade.

This is a guy who has been on more journeys, climbed more obstacles, and taken more risks to get where he is today than any person you probably know. When Branson talks, everyone listens. When Branson speaks, you are in for a load of inspiration.

The Stowe School, an independent school in Buckinghamshire, is where many would call Branson's educational beginnings. Stowe is where Branson decided to take a huge risk at sixteen years old and hope for the best: he dropped out.

After attending Stowe between 1963 and 1967, Branson jumped out into the world with his first business venture: *Student*, a political youth magazine.

From time to time, Branson returns to Stowe to deliver a speech full of knowledge and insight to young minds – to young persons who are sitting in the very same place the billionaire mogul of Virgin Group once sat himself.

After saying how good it feels to be back at Stowe, even if just for a visit, Branson went on to talk about how it is perfectly alright to not be cut out for academia.

Very clearly, determination is what Branson sees as getting a person further in life than book smarts: "It is great to be back. I have lots of happy memories. There are others, like myself, who weren't great academic, but are determined to get out there and live life to the fullest. Enjoy every minute of life and try to make a difference. Stowe has both sets or people and both sets of people can do well." [1]

Shortly after this inspirational anecdote, the business magnate admitted, playfully, that Stowe would have been more fun if it admitted girls. Apparently, one of the downsides for Branson attending Stowe was that it was an all-male school.

In endorsing Stowe School's decision to finally transform itself into co-educational, Branson said, "I think it's far more natural like this." [2]

CHAPTER 2: MOTIVATOR

When you're looking up at a man who took a chance so many people wouldn't have taken then made it work, without a doubt you know you're looking at a man who is full of those little inspirational phrases everybody needs to keep pushing ahead sometimes when you feel you're against the wind. Inspiring words can only come from inspiring people and Richard Branson can only be described as an inspiring person – nothing less.

Ideas are the foundation of his success. If a person doesn't come up with ideas, they probably won't get down the road and find themselves with success. Hey, that is just how life is for many of us.

However, you can't be afraid to think and you can't be afraid to let ideas come out of you. This is so much so that the mogul sees the importance in not getting stressed out over an idea. Let it out. Let it flow. See where it takes you.

However, Branson knows how hard it can be to do something that sounds so easy: "When you're first thinking through an idea, it's important to not get bogged down in complexity. Thinking simply and clearly, is hard to do." [3]

We have come to a point in this world where we judge people

for any little thing. In fact, people are often innocent before they are even remotely, possibly presumed to be innocent. Society operates in such a way to where a person's credibility is always on the fence in some way, to the point where people simply don't want to listen to anything that comes out of their mouth for certain reasons.

Branson is a guy who sees the flaw in this mode of thinking, as everyone is worth listening because something – yes, maybe just something – good will come out of anything they say. "Listen. Take the best. Leave the rest." [4] Branson obviously is an advocate for pulling out the good stuff, if nothing else.

Open mindedness is one of the must-have traits for anyone trying to be successful nowadays. Nothing can be further from the truth than for an entrepreneur. When you're out in the world, working for yourself, sometimes you have to get creative – sometimes you have to open your mind so you can see opportunities when they're staring you dead in the face.

Even more than that, Branson sees how a person has to be optimistic and do things simply because he or she wants to do them: "Entrepreneurial business favours the open mind. It favours people whose optimism drives them to prepare for many possible futures, pretty much purely for the joy of doing so." [5]

Anyone on this road of being open-minded and entrepreneurial knows that sometimes you just have to follow your gut. We live in a world where there is now this negative connotation to thinking with your emotions.

Business is quite the opposite regardless of how most people might actually see it. Your emotions can tell you a lot of things when you slow your brain down to actually listen to them. After all, emotions must be there for a reason and that reason could be to help you. Branson seems to think the same: "Engage your emotions at work. Your instincts and emotions are there to help you." [6]

Rolling with the punches is the only way you or anybody else is going to get to grab that oh-so-sweet feeling of success. Some of these punches are going to hurt. But if you're really in it for the long haul, this pain won't get you down.

That is the difference between those who will survive and those who will fall by the wayside then regret not getting back up years down the road. Branson surely knows all about this, as a part of business is failing and trying again.

Trying again is always moving ahead, no matter which way you look at it: "If you're hurt, lick your wounds and get up again. If you've given it your absolute best, it's time to move forward." [7]

Your emotions and the ability to stick through the pain of failing and trying again are what any entrepreneur needs to keep themselves going. In case you didn't know, this feeling will turn into that fire in your soul – that fire that keeps you inspired to make a difference and accomplish your goals.

The key to building this fire, though, is to let it grow so you can use it to get you even further, or at least that's how Branson sees it: "Entrepreneurship is about turning what excites you in life into capital, so what you can do more of it and move forward with it." [8]

Sure, there will be times where it seems easier to blame your wins and losses on chance. And yes, chance could very well be a factor in a lot of life – a lot more than we probably want to realize on a day-to-day basis.
However, the more prepared you are to take advantage of the positive things in life, Branson sees it as the better chance you will have to succeed: "Chance favours the prepared mine. The more you practice, the luckier you become." [9]

In case you didn't pick up on this, Branson is telling you is that you need to be the best at what you are trying to accomplish and always be prepared to turn a situation into a situation of good chance – a situation that works out in your favor.

While practice does make perfect and increases your chances, it also teaches you. There are many times in our lives where we are faced with being told that we're not qualified to fulfill the needs of a specific position.

Well, one of the great things about being an entrepreneur is that you really don't know what you're fit for until your head-deep, swimming in it – kind of like if you moved to Peru to learn Spanish rather than learning it from classes, or at least that is what Branson would probably think:

"The best way of learning about anything is by doing." If you want to learn how the Roman's do, you've got to go to Rome and learn. It sure doesn't seem like Branson trusts everything he finds on Google.

CHAPTER 3: SWASHBUCKLING

Do you know anybody who uses the word swashbuckling? Most people probably don't know a single soul who would ever dare to use the word swashbuckling. Branson uses the word, and the business mogul is obvious a big advocate for taking a chance and getting out of the cubicle if that is what your heart is telling you to do:

"If you want swashbuckling action in your life, become an entrepreneur and give it a go." [10] Don't become complacent; don't settle. That's all Branson is trying to get across to you.

Everybody wants everything cheap. Hey, who are we kidding? You want it fast too. Wal-Mart; McDonalds; high-speed Wi-Fi. All of these things and many more that we take for granted on a day-to-day basis are because society has gotten to a point where we want everything fast and we want it to be cheap.

However, doing things for these reasons, at least in Branson's eyes, just might be a bad idea: "Don't think what's the cheapest way to do it or what's the fastest way to do it ... think 'what's the most amazing way to do it."

Basically, do stuff for the art of doing it. Don't do it for the end result or because you're trying to save a buck and some time. In many ways, this goes back to that age-old saying: anything worth doing is worth doing well. [11]

CHAPTER 4: MAKING BUSINESS FUN

If whatever business you choose isn't exercising your mind, you just might be in that business for the wrong reasons. Missteps like these wears on a person's mentality after a while; they crush your soul. This is so much so that the feeling you get is that same feeling when you ignore your instinct, forgetting that instincts are built into the human psyche for a reason.

Everything about a business has to use your mind and you as a person have to enjoy it – two things which probably helped Branson to become the mega-success that he is today: "A business has to be involving, it has to be fun, and it has to exercise your creative instincts." [12]

Branson is all about making business fun. Let's face it: you've got to have a vision so you can have a competitive edge. It is what it is. No pain, no glory. You have to look at an opportunity, market, or industry and see what you can do to come on the scene and change the game – change the game in a way where your mark will forever be left on it when you're gone:

"I've had great fun turning quite a lot of different industries on their head and making sure those industries will never be the same again, because Virgin went in and took them on." [13]

Business is a warzone. And you've got to have strategy when you're stepping onto that battlefield. Well, Branson certainly has all the strategy he needs. If his successes don't speak loud enough for themselves, maybe it's the fact that the business mogul saw that he'd need to overcome his poor spelling:

"Although my spelling is still sometimes poor, I have managed to overcome the world of my difficulties through training myself to concentrate." [14]
Focus, people. Focus!
Sometimes, to be successful in business you have to really not see yourself as a businessman. Don't get into that mindset of limiting yourself. Branson keeps the joy in what he does by not really looking at is as business, and this includes the airline industry:
"If I was a businessman, or saw myself as a businessman, I would have never gone into the airline business." [15]

Yeah, it may be a little hard to figure out what he's saying at first. Give it a little thought. Come back to it. You will find that he is letting his creative mind run wild rather than thinking of his every move as a business, for a businessman might have stayed away from the airline industry due to the risks involved.

Independence is a must-have for anyone trying to finally get their piece of the pie out in this cold world. Most of us aren't born to families who were feeding us with silver spoons, and neither was Branson.

In fact, he was born to rather humble beginnings. Because of these beginnings, Branson can recall values his mother instilled in him as a little boy that got him ready to be on the road to being what he is today:

"My mother was determined to make us independent. When I was four years old, she stopped the car a few miles from our house and made me find my own way homes across the fields. I got hopelessly lost." [16]

Hey, tough love never hurt anybody, did it?

If nothing else, Branson learned that as part of having a vision, not only do you have to be willing to go after it, but you also have to be willing to articulate the vision. Put a timed expiration on it.

Make it seem as real to you and your future as the air you breathe. Then maybe – just maybe – you'll have a better chance of it coming true: "We believe that within five years, 96 percent of British consumers will have access to the internet, whether it be through a personal computer, a set-top box, or a mobile phone." [17]

This vision came true for Branson, as you can see. Do you really have to read up on whether or not what he predicted at this time has come true?

CHAPTER 5: EXPERIMENTING

Experimenting is the key to success. The more you experiment, the better chance you have at finding something that will stick and pay off in the long run. Don't focus on trying to plan everything out.

Sure, some stuff needs planning. However, with a lot of things you just have to follow your gut and see what the heck happens. Branson gets it: "You'll never know with these things when you're trying something new that can happen. This is all experimental." [18]

Keep your head high and your expectations of yourself even higher, but don't get your hopes too far up. If nothing else, when it finally happens for you, you'll be just as surprised as the next person.

There is nothing wrong with being involved in something. In fact, being involved is a great way to get your feet wet, learn the ropes, and take whatever it is you've learned or seen to your own ventures.

Knowledge is indeed power. Branson sees how being a part of something, if nothing else, is a great way to make a difference by bringing something to the table – by leaving your mark in some way while you learn: "We'd love to be involved with the creation of something very special, something quite large, and something quite exciting." [19]

No matter what you do, though, you have got to go hard or go home. Be competitive for God's sake. It is perfectly fine to look at what somebody else has done and make it your personal mission to do better than that person in whatever way you possibly can.

What would a guy like Branson think of records? "Records are made to be broken. It is a man's nature to continue to strive to do just that." [20]

CHAPTER 6: MATERIAL THINGS

No matter what you do, don't be in it for the sake of material possessions. Sure, it's easy to get the impression that material things are all that wealthy guys like Branson are in the game for, but in reality nothing could be further from the truth for Branson:
"Ridiculous yachts and private planes and big limousines won't make people enjoy life more, and it sends out terrible messages to people who work for them. It would be so much better if that money was spent in Africa and it's about getting a balance." [21]

Find a little purpose because purpose is what will really help you to enjoy your life. Think about what you're telling the people who work for you – the people you inspire being you and enjoyable to be around.

Pride isn't just something that men have, but it is a part of basic human nature. Don't look at the end result in terms of how much money you made. Stay clear of caring for one mini-second about the praise of another human being, simply because people will love you when you're up then hate you when you're down.

Branson's philosophy of business has always been built around this very principal: "Above all, you want to create something you're proud of. This has always been my philosophy of business.

I can honestly say that I have never gone into any business purely to make money. If that is the sole motive, then I believe you are better off not doing it." [22]

Hey, don't beat yourself up about things. Everybody does it, from the guy who picks up the trash every morning before dawn to that stiff in the suit downtown throwing up funny hand gestures to traders and other stock brokers clustering around on the floor like bees in a hornet's nest:

"I don't think of work as work and play as play. It's all living." [23] Okay, so obviously Branson doesn't get worked up over things. Take one thing at a time and enjoy every second of it, because it is all living.

CHAPTER 7: DELEGATION

Knowing how to play up your strengths and down your weaknesses is important to success as an entrepreneur. And let's face it, there will be times, whether you like it or not, where you will have to move out of the way, even with your own business, and let someone else take the wheel.

Sure, this isn't easy to do. A lot of people struggle with it, in fact. However, for a man even as powerful as Branson, he too knows when it is time to practice the oh-so-needed art of delegation:

"As much as you need a strong personality to build a business from scratch, you also must understand the art of delegation. I have to be good at helping people run the individual businesses, and I have to be willing to step back. The company must be set up so it can continue without me." 24

If you've made good choices in the past, and put the right person in the right places, a business will be able to do just that – a business will be able to run without you. Hint: this is your chance to kick back on a beach with something good to drink and watch the clouds roll right on by while the cold water splashes your toes.

While you're resting, or cooking up your next opportunity, don't sweat it if some other opportunities pass by. It happens! Chill out. Maybe – just maybe – it wasn't meant to be.

Life is full of opportunities and sometimes you just have to be in the right place at the right time with the right mindset, or at least that is how Branson sees it. This is one business mogul who compares business opportunities to buses:

"Business opportunities are like buses, there's always another one coming." [25]

Many people will tell you that if you're thinking of starting a business, think about getting an accountant to help you handle your business affairs. More importantly, if nothing else, get one so you don't get into trouble with Uncle Sam. Nobody in this whole wide world can take on the IRS.

However, Branson doesn't suggest you get an accountant involved before the business is up and going: "I never get the accountants in before I start up a business. It's done on gut feeling, especially if I can see they are taking a mickey out of the consumer." [26]

If your gut isn't telling you to get an accountant, don't be one of those people you know who are always trying to fix something that isn't broken.

Being an entrepreneur is about climbing mountains – about setting goals for yourself and seeing how far you can rise above them. If Richard Branson didn't have this kind of mindset, how in the world would he be able to go on to have a billion-dollar empire like Virgin?

He lets his interests push him forward: "My interests in life come from setting myself huge, apparently unachievable challenges and trying to rise above them." [27] If this were a tweet, it would be viral on the internet with #riseabove on the end.

Finally, sometimes you just have to step back and take a look around when it's all said and done. Give yourself a chance to be grateful for what you do have – grateful for what you have accomplished.

Remember to not take it for granted, but to simply enjoy maybe giving yourself a pat on the back for the simple things life. And by simple, Branson means truly simple: "Right now, I'm just happy to be alive and to have had a nice hot bath." [28]

CHAPTER 8: TEAM BUILDING

No entrepreneur is truly out in the warzone alone. In fact, nothing is further from the truth. Gone are the days of being the wealthy recluse who lives up in a big, fancy house that overlooks the city from the hills.

Nonetheless, there are people in the world who are under the impression that an entrepreneur acts and operates alone. There are people who think these persons only need and use their personality to overcome challenges or bring his or her own idea to a market or industry. If that is what you thought, get it out of your head as quickly as possible because you've got it all wrong.

Few successful people in business – well, almost no successful people in business – have been able to achieve anything in life without help. For this reason, and many more, Richard Branson sees why it is so very important to understand the art of team-building.

It is so easy to make the wrong choice when you're in that team building phase of your life, career, or business empire. The first thing to get right, according to Branson, is to "never say I'm the boss."

Branson talks about in his own book *Like a Virgin: Secrets*

They Won't Teach You at Business School, how being bossy just isn't a trait of real leaders. To be bossy, in Branson's eyes, is to simply bark orders. Real leaders do not bark. Real leaders organize – they motivate, they inspire.

Rather, Branson sees another way to be more of a team-player while being a leader. He hates when people give in and just say, "Okay, fine. You're the boss." [29]

To Branson, this is simply telling him that he hasn't got a team, but rather a throne where people are only doing what he says because he said it even if it is an idea that probably sucks.

In an *Entrepreneur* blog post, Branson is quoted as addressing his advice for team-building: "don't restrict creative freedom." [30]

Even for a man with so much power, the creative freedoms of those who work either for him or work on his team are one of the most important assets of doing business. Branson understands how a company should act to get the best and most positive energy out of a person on its team:

"You need to give your people the freedom to get creative, to come up with their own ideas and run with them. If someone comes to you with an idea for a business, why not ask that person to launch a startup? Over the years, some of our employees' ideas have resulted in our setting up businesses. This has helped us to enter new markets and, more often than not, succeed. Your company should act as a springboard for ambitious employees, not a set of shackles." [31]

CHAPTER 9: TAKE A STEP BACK

Part of being a successful entrepreneur, to Branson, as you know, is being able to step back. Sometimes when you do just that, you can spot a problem and do something about the problem before it becomes a real headache that will have you reaching for that bottle of aspirin in the middle of the day or taking your blood pressure when you get home in the evening:

"There is nothing efficient about allowing a small problem to escalate." [32]

To Branson, sending out text messages or emails is not a good way to go about handling situations. Yes, even this very busy man believes in picking up the phone and calling someone. Better yet, he will get up and walk right on over to that person's office and address the situation face-to-face. This saves time, and a heck of a lot of potential misunderstandings.

Nobody likes an asshole, even in business. These kinds of people can make the people they work with, for, and or around just feel uncomfortable. And we all know that when people are uncomfortable, they are far more likely to make bad, or wrong, decisions. One rule for Branson when it comes to team-building is: "never make a team member uncomfortable." [33]

Making people feel uncomfortable is one quick-fire way to sap someone's drive to be the best – to contribute their best to the task at hand: "It takes an engaged, motivated and committed workforce to deliver a first-class product or service and build a successful, sustainable enterprise." [34]

Do you see what I mean! That guy a few offices down, or downstairs at the cubicle by the water fountain, needs to be just as comfortable as the guys in suits at the CEO table.

CHAPTER 10: POINTING FINGERS

Branson says, "Don't point fingers." [35]

When Branson's Virgin Atlantic's inaugural flight was forced to make an emergency landing in 1984 after just one minute into the flight because the engine was exploding, the first thing he wanted to do was look around and blame someone.

Come on, this is just a basic human instinct for a lot of people. Did something go wrong? It is not my fault; it is his fault. Yeah, that guy over there. As a leader, Branson has realized, you have got to remember to not point fingers – to not place blame. Rather, use all of that energy on handling whatever is going down and finding a solution so it isn't likely to happen again.

A rule of Branson's is: "don't back away from a debate." [36] Part of being successful, especially in business, is to never back down. Yes, many of the same rules that apply in the "streets" go for business as well, and this would definitely be one of them.

Through his five decades in business, Branson has definitely learned the ins and outs of a healthy debate and how it affects the long-term strategy: "Over almost 50 years in business, I have learned that having a healthy debate about strategy and direction is vital if a business is to succeed, so I always encourage my colleagues to challenge me and speak up if they disagree with any of our group's plans."

When it comes to team-building, each person at the table needs to be given the opportunity to voice their opinion and challenge others. As the old saying goes: we can just agree to disagree. One of Branson's most famous quotes is about going toe-to-toe with someone in a debate is: "Screw it, let's do it." [37]

CHAPTER 11: TAKING NOTES

There is one rule for team-building that Branson has figured out that might be hard for a lot of people to see: "Don't be invisible." [38] Think about it! You see Richard Branson, out and about. Between New York, Los Angeles, and even Australia, his name, face, and brand have personally touched many a-shores around the world.

A common practice of the business mogul is to bring with him a notebook when meeting customers and employees. Branson makes points of not only what makes them happy, but also their ideas.

When you get out of your comfort zone and go out and really market yourself, not only are you selling yourself, but you are also making your business known and you're collecting plenty of good ideas from people – people who have just-as-valuable input, if your ears and mind are open and listening.

Maybe you remember your mother and father telling you this, but Richard Branson lives by this idea when it comes to team-building: "never burn bridges." [39]
This simply means don't go out into the world ending relationships on a bad note. It also applies to partnerships and employees. These are two things that, if you stay in the game long enough, will change with the times. And there is absolutely nothing wrong with this!

Funny story: one time Branson wore a flight attendant's uniform. Sound familiar? [hint: cover of this book] How many billionaires do you know that would slide into a flight attendant's uniform?

Anyway, the reason Branson did this was because he had lost a bet to a former employee who turned competitor. Branson believes that in place of burning bridges with a member of your team, or a partner, try to part ways smoothly.

The more amicable you can make it, the better. Wish the person the best of luck. This is not only in a professional sense, but these kinds of gestures also leave the doors wide open for you to be able to work with the person again in the future. Hey, you never know when you're going to need someone again. Never assume you won't.

CHAPTER 12: EXERCISE BOTH MIND AND BODY

While team building is part of being efficient, don't for a second underestimate the power of being productive. Think about it! Business makes all sorts of decisions all the time in the name of increasing productivity.

There is absolutely no way that Richard Branson would see the kind of success he has seen with Virgin if the guy wasn't living the definition of productivity. After all, to start more than 400 companies, if nothing else, is a sign that the man isn't lazy or just waiting around for something to be handed to him.

Believe it or not, "exercise" is one of Richard Branson's secrets to being productive. You have to keep things going. And part of keeping things going, first must start with you keeping yourself going. Everybody knows that exercising increases your levels of energy.

Exercise also helps you sleep better – sleep you will need when you're an entrepreneur – and that sleep even goes as far as improving your focus and concentration. Branson gets up literally at the crack of dawn – 6 a.m. – to run.

Make a list. Remember your mom telling you that? Maybe you remember her doing just that before you all hopped in the car to head over to the grocery store. Either way, lists are a great way of being efficient and increasing productivity.

Branson says, "I have always lived my life by making lists: lists of people to call, list of ideas, lists of companies to set up, lists of people who can make things happen. Each day I work through these lists, and that sequence of calls propels me forward." [40]

You've got to love what you do, above everything else, to truly be a productive person. To do this, gear your focus toward things you actually enjoy – toward things that you really like to do and are good at. Everything else, according to Richard Branson? "Delegate. Outsource." [41]

CHAPTER 13: NEGOTIATION

Negotiation has been a crucial part of the game Richard Branson has played to get where he is at this point. However, to be good at negotiating, Branson has had to perfect is own skills of listening – a skill which far too many people, particularly people with power, lack:

"My ability to listen to the other people and accept it when their suggestions are better than mine has been useful during my 40 years in business. I'm never too proud to admit I'm wrong or take action when others' suggestions are better." [42]

Branson doesn't believe in taking things personally, either. After all, the saying "don't take it personal" has to exist for a reason. To Branson, the uphill battle that is the climb of success is indeed treacherous, but it is important to remember to have fun:

"Remember to have fun. There is no point in being in business if it is not fun. Have fun with your team, your suppliers and the companies you work with. It is so much more rewarding to build up rapport than to find yourself in a constant battle. Don't take everything so personally. Let your hair down now and again. And have some fun. Look at me – it's a philosophy that has served me well for 40 years!" [43]

Anyone in Branson's shoes would have all the insight you

could ever need in the world about negotiation. Sure, you can be locked down to the final hour, trying to think of what strategy would work best for you; for everybody; for the sake of your business.

However, to Branson at least, if you want to be good at negotiation, teamwork can often be the way to win: "The key is to remain calm and collected. If you are getting angry, take a deep breath, realize you are taking it too personally and, even, take a step back. Rely on those around you to help you out. Teamwork can often win."

CHAPTER 14: CRUISES

Branson has plenty of experience when it comes to negotiation for his own business, Virgin Cruises. This particular vision has faced many obstacles, but recent news announced that Virgin Cruises would take three ships that are capable of carrying 3,000 passengers each starting in early 2020: "It's no secret I've dreamed of building a cruise line for a very long time." [44]

The obstacles about this venture deal with having been in the form of a $300 million lawsuit by former CEO of Norwegian Cruise Line Holdings, Colin Veitch. Veitch oversaw Norwegian from 2000 to 2008, and in the lawsuit he claims that Virgin squeezed him out of his plan to enter the very profitable cruise industry.

In usual Branson fashion, however, he steps up to the controversy and remains calm about the situation: "We're fully confident the lawsuit doesn't have any merit." [45]

CHAPTER 15: REORGANIZE, DON'T FIRE

When dealing with other people, a difficult thing to do for many people, including Branson, is to look beyond your own feelings: "It's often hard to get past your own feelings of frustration when dealing with others. Delegating to a member of your team brings a fresh pair of eyes and often a different approach and perspective." [46]

This goes back to the benefit of good teamwork, even when negotiating. Just think of the old saying: two heads are better than one. Truer words have never been spoken, even when it comes to business.

Branson clearly understands the value of human resources. With his ability to step back, without a doubt the utmost importance is to put on getting the right butts in the right seats so the business can run smoothly when Branson isn't around.

However, when he is around, the business mogul sees the importance of surrounding himself with a management team that compliments him and his objectives in business overall: "One of my key lessons over the years has been to surround myself with great management teams who complement me and ensure that we have the all-around skills to make our businesses succeed." [47]

No matter how well you think you've placed the right person in the right position, there will still come a time when you simply need to go a different direction with the said person. We live in a society where if an employee is not good at one particular position, they are labeled as not being good for anything and are not really given the opportunity to shine – to be in a position where they can really show their capabilities. Branson, himself, doesn't believe in just firing people:

"If a member of your team is not performing as you expect, don't write him or her off immediately. At Virgin if an employee is not doing well in one area, I feel that he or she should be given the opportunity to try out in a different Virgin job.

Firing people should never be your first option. In some cases, when letting people go is your only option, prepare for the conversation with constructive suggestions about why it is not working out and other ideas the employee should pursue. That will help make the process easier for both of you." [48]

CHAPTER 16: OPTIMISTIC THINKING

One common mistake business owners make in negotiating with people on all levels is being too aggressive. Sure, it is so easy to get carried away trying to follow your vision that you simply forget or put to the side how you may be coming across to people.

However, Branson sees it as nothing but to your benefit to do all of this without being aggressive: "There are lots of ways to get your point across and make your business successful without being aggressive. Always remember that you love what you do and your role is to persuade others to love your business, too, and, therefore, to want to work with you.

You can negotiate competitively without aggression. Understand what you want to achieve and what leverage you possess to help you reach your goals. Less aggression and more determination is what you need." [49]

Being socially inclusive is becoming a major part of running a successful business in today's world. With the onset of globalization in recent years, more and more different nationalities, mindsets, and ways of life are now at the business table dressed in suits like everybody else.

Without a doubt, when running the more than 400 companies that make up Virgin, Branson has to be remindful to himself of the value of everyone – the value of being inclusive: "I hope we are successful at Virgin because we engage with everyone in a positive, inclusive manner rather than in an aggressive, combative or negative way." [50]

Branson even sees an advantage in having a couple of drinks after work to calm down from stress – stress from either the human resources aspect of business, or stress from the gruesome nature of negotiating.

In this end, however, he trusts his ability to lean back and trust the system that is in place – trust the team and let them do what they are capable of doing while you take a couple of shots and relax:

"I often find, after a tough set of talks, that it is good to go out for a drink or two and get it off your chest! You may have a sore head in the morning but relying on and confiding in your team will often help you put everything in perspective." [51]

CHAPTER 17: RAILROADS

What is so great about a guy like Richard Branson is not only is he a visionary, but the man can also step back and loose at a business model then tell you what is and what is not working about the model. Branson has even been able to do this when it comes to Network Rail.

The United Kingdom's largest network of rails is operated by Network Rail and Branson sees that the company is too big and should definitely be divided into regional branches so the business can be more efficient: "Network Rail is far too big a company. I think that companies that kind of size should be broken up into small units." [52]

Why does Network Rail and what they do even a concern of the Virgin tycoon? Well, Virgin also operates on these very same tracks and feels the ripple effects of non-efficiency. His customers are feeling the issues, so he is feeling the issues.

Like any good business man, rather than placing blame, he traced the route of the problem right back to its stem: "We get enormously frustrated that people say will say that Virgin Rail has delays, but 90% of those delays are down to Network Rail. If we were running the track underneath, because we've got out trains running on that track we'd make absolutely certain that track was fixed and running well, because we value our reputation." [53]

Richard Branson isn't afraid to throw his ideas into the atmosphere, either. And you would think with as much experience and success as he has had that people would listen and take what he has to say into consideration. When asked if he thought that a Network Rail break-up was likely, Branson said, "I don't know, I've thrown that idea out before. Maybe right now it's an option that might be considered." 54

CHAPTER 18: RACE CARS

Richard Branson has even given a little of his wisdom from his plethora of ventures to the racing industry. While the racing industry is indeed a billion-dollar industry, Branson sees ways it can improve in the future.

The Virgin tycoon let the world know that he thinks all-electric and solar-powered racing cars would attract more sponsors. Even furthermore, Branson believes that these kinds of cars would attract race-car fanatics within the next several years.

Branson is obviously a fan of the new Formula E racing development of electric vehicles. He suggested that the pace for developing them was so rapid that Formula E's all-electric series would soon pass up Formula 1 as the main choice for sponsors and fans. Branson already has a vision ahead of the United Kingdom's first ever 100% electric motor car race in London about EV's potential to "seriously disrupt the automobile industry" [55]

"I think there is still going to be room for Formula 1 in the next few years, but four or five years from now you will see Formula E overtaking Formula 1. Just as clean energy type of businesses will power ahead of other types of businesses." [56]

Branson is even "willing to bet" on his visions, the sign of a man who is truly confident in his business skills. From his point of view, within just a couple of decades there will be no new vehicles that are not powered by electric battery – that there would be none made in the world.

Branson let the world see what he sees in his crystal ball: "The current technology is antiquated and polluting and will disappear. Like other sectors, everything will be clean and companies that move quickest in that area are going to dominate the marketplace." [57]

With Formula E, Branson even sees a "revolution" in the world's future. Just like how Branson's rule is to set a goal that seems impossible to pass, just that has happened with Formula E. The series will push clean technology to the limit:

"Ten or 20 years ago, people might have thought electric cars were what granny drove, but now they see wonderful hybrids, Elon Musk's cars, or Formula E vehicles going 140mph around the track. I think it will spur on the revolution the world needs." [58]

CHAPTER 19: AIRLINE COMPETITION

In case you didn't know, a bit of a turf war was raging between Virgin Australia and Qantas Airways. The battle was initiated by Virgin Australia against Qantas Airways, and has caused both business entities to lose a lot of money. Here, Branson has even expressed regret over how the situation has been handled, calling it "foolish."

Branson owns a 10 percent part in the Australian airline that operates under the Virgin umbrella, but even he can see how Australians are better off by what all has transpired because the competition increased by Qantas response being extremely aggressive – by Qantas adding two planes for every one extra Virgin had in the market.

Shares soared once the smoke cleared. However, Branson compares it to a boxing match: "It was like a boxing match where there was no real winner." 59

Now, however, Branson can step back and learn from the entire turf war over airspace above Australia. It came to a point where Branson realized that indeed the town was big enough for the both of them, so to speak, and that he had to let the chips fall where they may:

"We were beating each other to a pulp but neither of us were going to go anyway and it cost both companies hundreds of millions. Finally, some sense has prevailed. It was just foolish. I think they [Qantas] genuinely thought they could push us over the cliff, and when they realised they couldn't push us over the cliff they gave it one last attempt by ringing the government and asking for a billion or two to try and finish Virgin off. For a second I thought the government was going to make a really foolish decision and oblige them, [but] they backed off." [60]

Branson admitted that during the war, Virgin lost a whopping $49 million in the previous financial year. However, this did not scare Branson one bit, as he was not the least bit interested in selling his stake of the company.

In fact, he was happy with the direction the airline took under someone on its team: chief executive John Borghetti. Even Qantas posted a profit that year, which Branson saw as a bluff:

"They came out with good figures and I think it was a hell of a bluff, which fortunately the government saw through. The travelling public have of course benefited from all this. Qantas has got a bit better as a result of Virgin Australia." [61]

In his belief of good teamwork, when it comes to the Qantas turf war, Branson knew when to put his gun away and work with the powers that be for a common good. Branson pitched his global satellite venture to the Coalition government while visiting Australia. Branson's main goal is to offer an alternative to NBN, or National Broadband Network.

As you can see from what he says, Branson goes at the situation with very little aggression and with his ears and eyes wide open: "We will be talking to Malcolm Turnbull about how we can help Australia connect everybody at a price that will save the taxpayer billions. Australia has embarked on trying to connect everybody in Australia.

That is not realistic. It is incredibly expensive for Australia to reach the last 20 percent of people. OneWeb can come in and give people Wi-Fi internet access for a fraction of the price than the government can do it with their current plans." [62]

CHAPTER 20: HOTELS AND MONEY

Branson also has is eyes on Australia to expand Virgin's global portfolio of hotels. He told the *Australian Financial Review* that the continent/country would indeed be a "natural place" to develop his brand in the hotel market.

Virgin has also considered bringing the new Virgin Sport business to Australia and has met with senior executives from Bank of Queensland to explore ways the Virgin Money business can benefit the Australian market:

"Virgin Money has been the most successful challenger brand in the UK and we would like that to be the case in Australia. Small businesses love Virgin so maybe we could get into small business loans." [63]

CHAPTER 21: CONNECTING THE U.K. AND AUSTRALIA

Leave it up to Branson to have a vision that involves connecting Australia with its motherland, the United Kingdom. Now in existence is what is known as Virgin Galactic long-haul flight plans.

One of Richard Branson's predictions is that within a generation or two, it will be totally possible to fly from Australia to London in less than two hours. And Branson is already making moves to try to make it happen:

"I think in my children's lifetime you'll definitely be able to fly London to Australia in the air, I think you could be less than two hours. By the time you've got through airport etcetera, it could be more like four or five hours. But the flight itself could be really quick." [64]

Even Branson realized when he had to downsize his vision just a tad bit, as Virgin Galactic's initial idea was to focus on space tourism – tourism where the wealthy would fork out to the tune of $US200,000 for a ride.

Branson sees how other technologies would be helpful to the overall dream of Virgin Galactic and how they have changed over the last several decades. However, Branson himself has been involved in one of those changes: the development of the Boeing 787 Dreamliner.

In the name of efficiency and productivity, saving oil was one of the main goals: "We flew a plane around the world non-stop, the Virgin Atlantic Global Flyer, with Steve Fossett flying it some years ago. It was made of all carbon-composite material in an attempt to try to show Boeing and Airbus, look, you can build planes with carbon fibre which will save a lot of fuel. Now you've got the (Airbus) A350 and the 787 plane which are made largely of carbon composite material. That means they're using a lot less fuel, which is good for the environment and good for the travelling public because it keeps fares down." [65]

CHAPTER 22: BRANSON, MISSOURI

Branson, Missouri is probably an easy place to overlook. Sure, it's famous in a lot of ways. It is a well-known place in Missouri for having things to do and tourism and whatnot. However, when people think about where to invest in Missouri, Kansas City and St. Louis probably come to mind first. Well, maybe people even think of Springfield down in the lower left corner of the state.

Interestingly enough, Richard Branson himself has found that his family tree reaches back to the early days of Branson. And now the billionaire eyes opportunities in the region of the state known as the Ozarks:

"I may have started 400 companies, but my great-uncle Ruben S. Branson founded a city." This is in response to information from the White River Valley Historical Society.

Branson's' uncle founded the city of Branson in 1882. There, he owned a general store and post office that were the first registered addresses of the city: "Now that I have traced our lineage to Branson, I'm excited to find out more. From Dolly Parton's Dixie Stampede to the stunning Ozark Mountains, Branson puts the Show in the Show Me State." [66]

Very few business moguls of Branson's stature actually take the time to read up and research on investing in somewhere with some sentimental meaning. Even better than this, Branson cares about the growth of the town his ancestor started: "...exploring opportunities in Branson, Missouri – want to paint the town red." Of course, Branson welcomes their "offspring" with open arms and is looking forward to any changes and investments the British billionaire has in store. [67]

CHAPTER 23: VIETNAM VISIT

Branson, Missouri isn't the only region Richard Branson has his eyes on. The business mogul is always eager to offer up some advice to various regions on what they can do to put themselves in a better economic position. Well, for Branson, in a strange way, he has a connection to Vietnam.

The magazine he quit high school to start, *Student*, was what he hoped he could use to change the world. In this magazine, Branson protested the Vietnam War. Now, more than five decades later, the business mogul decided to visit Vietnam. His goal was to tell the people that they too could change the world in a different way – through free enterprise.

Branson attended a conference in Ho Chi Minh City where he stressed how professional success can come to you in many ways. However, he sees community as an important part of business as well: "But people who reach success as business leaders have a responsibility to invest their money in their community." [68]

In front of an audience of 7,000 people, Branson uttered the words, "You've got to make sure you use that money to tackle problems in your community, in your country." [69]

It is worth mentioning that the Vietnamese saw Branson for the business genius that he is and considered anything he said an inspiration. In a country where the annual per capita income is $2,000, there were people who paid as much as $3,500 to attend the function and meet with Branson.

Branson took a moment to reflect on Vietnam's history and showed understanding of why the nation would be reluctant to try new economic models. However, a lot of Vietnam does indeed already accept capitalism. It was found that 95 percent of Vietnamese are seeing that the people of Vietnam are living better quality of life in a free market economy.

Branson said that he "hoped Vietnam's rising business leaders would use their wealth and power for social causes." In regards to how Vietnam's change from communism to free markets only began as recently as the 1980s, Branson says, "Everything is new in Vietnam. So in Vietnam really we have to learn the new model from another country.

From Singapore or the USA or Europe. We have to learn new things, the updated things." [70] Just by the sheer tone in his voice, and how he uses the word 'we,' the billionaire feels invested in the very country just forty years before he helped protest the war through his first business venture.

CHAPTER 24: GIVING BACK

Giving back to his own community is exactly what Branson is up to nowadays. His goal now is to just keep on giving back. In 2015, he started a competition offering $1 million prizes for what are called "disruptive start-ups."

The annual, nationwide competitive, called Pitch to Rich, was made with the idea in mind of supporting innovative and daring entrepreneurs who have the guts, and the ideas, to make a difference in the world – to change the game.

The goal of Pitch to Rich is to find the best up-and-coming start-ups and reward them with the opportunity of a lifetime: a chance to pitch for investment from Sir Richard Branson, as he is widely known across the United Kingdom. Pitch to Rich is looking for the undiscovered talent – the talent of entrepreneur and businesses that show the Virgin spirt of enterprise.

One major contest rule shows Branson's dedication to his community: entrants must be UK residents with a UK based business and aged 18 years or over. What did Branson have to say about Pitch to Rich?

"Launching a business can be challenging and, at times, overwhelming. But entrepreneurs shouldn't let this hold them back from achieving their full potential. Pitch to Rich is a brilliant opportunity for UK businesses to make their mark on a global stage. If you think your business has great potential, then enter Pitch to Rich today, as you never know where it may lead you." [71]

CHAPTER 25: CONCLUSION

Branson is an inspiration, with inspiration being a gross understatement. The man has guts. The man has talent. This London-native has been able to turn negatives into positive and use that same energy to perceiver even when the odds were against him.

As an exemplification of braveness, Richard Branson shows just about anyone just how far they can make it in the world if they change and tweak a few things about their thinking.

Through Branson, the true entrepreneur can learn that it is perfectly okay to not be an academic whiz. After all, Branson himself was not one. And he doesn't regret it, nor does he consider his time in school a waste of his time.

To put it simply, the man learned something even from his educational experience at Stowe. Now, he gets to go back and reflect – he gets to go back and let new eyes and minds learn from him that they have options.

Branson has an inspirational quote for just about everything, showing that he has learned a little something here and a little something there from every step he has taken on his journey. He has condensed the information down to sentence or two lines that anyone can look at to start their day – to start their minds – and keep their feet rolling toward their objective of success.

However, even Branson recognizes that none of his success would be remotely possible if he were alone. Even he himself admits how extremely unlikely such a feat would be, and can offer up plenty of information on just how to meet the right people; how to keep the right people around you; and how to respect the views of and pull from people around you. Good team-building leads to excellent productivity.

And excellent productivity will help an entrepreneur get right on their way to success because everyone is doing everything that he or she should be doing, including you.

Negotiation is an art, and it is an art that you will be tested in when doing business. Branson himself had to learn the art of negotiation and how powerful of a tool being good and well-versed in the practice can be. The man has been faced with multi-million dollar lawsuits over his vision to have Virgin Cruises embark out of Miami, but even the fear of the quick swoop of a gavel hasn't slowed him down.

And who ever thought Australian airspace would create such a fuss? Whether or not it was thought out, Branson keeps pushing until a solution is reached that is good for the common good. He even sees how the completion with Qantas was good for the Australian people and chalked up the losses and kept it moving.

Through his many years in business, Branson has learned the value of keeping it cool, not getting too caught up on things, and keeping your eye open for another bus, or opportunity, rather.

When it comes to places outside of his desk, you never know where Branson's eye could be drawn to next. Whether you see it as purely coincidental, or as a sign of fate, Branson, Missouri has popped up on Branson's radar. A little family history digging showed his connection to the Missouri town and now the Ozarks region will get a little benefit from his vision and wisdom.

This is a man who dropped out of school at 16 years old to start his first venture, *Student*. And while he hasn't looked back for ways to go back and finish his education, Vietnam now has a special significance to him – a place with no family ties.

To Richard Branson, Vietnam is simply a geographic interest, shall we say, that has now led him to giving a little inspiration and business wisdom to the nation on how they can transform fully and successfully from communism to a free market economy.

Finally, back at home, Branson has given back to his community in many ways, a practice that is important, according to him, for any person in business. Through his wisdom, Branson has given a little insight on how Network Rail can increase its efficiency and what these kinds of actions would do for the United Kingdom as a whole.

Through his ideas of team building and delegating, he recommends that the large network be broken into smaller parts. Do you see a little efficiency and a better means of productivity in that idea?

Branson is also trying to help Britain's up and coming entrepreneurs get their feet in the door and their shoes wet through his Pitch to Rich competition. Young business men and women get the chance to pitch an idea to Branson himself with the opportunity of getting investment help and advice.

You just can't beat this, especially when the advice and help from one of your own people and is up close and personal.

FOOTNOTES

1. http://www.stowe.co.uk/news-and-events/news-archive/151/sir-richard-branson-returns-to-stowe
2. http://www.stowe.co.uk/news-and-events/news-archive/151/sir-richard-branson-returns-to-stowe
3. http://www.virgin.com/entrepreneur/10-inspirational-richard-branson-quotes
4. http://www.virgin.com/entrepreneur/10-inspirational-richard-branson-quotes
5. http://www.virgin.com/entrepreneur/10-inspirational-richard-branson-quotes
6. http://www.virgin.com/entrepreneur/10-inspirational-richard-branson-quotes
7. http://www.virgin.com/entrepreneur/10-inspirational-richard-branson-quotes
8. http://www.virgin.com/entrepreneur/10-inspirational-richard-branson-quotes
9. http://www.virgin.com/entrepreneur/10-inspirational-richard-branson-quotes
10. http://www.virgin.com/entrepreneur/10-inspirational-richard-branson-quotes
11. http://www.virgin.com/entrepreneur/10-inspirational-richard-branson-quotes
12. http://www.virgin.com/entrepreneur/richard-bransons-top-20-virgin-inspirational-insights
13. http://www.virgin.com/entrepreneur/richard-bransons-top-20-virgin-inspirational-insights

14. http://www.virgin.com/entrepreneur/richard-bransons-top-20-virgin-inspirational-insights

15. http://www.virgin.com/entrepreneur/richard-bransons-top-20-virgin-inspirational-insights

16. http://www.virgin.com/entrepreneur/richard-bransons-top-20-virgin-inspirational-insights

17. http://www.virgin.com/entrepreneur/richard-bransons-top-20-virgin-inspirational-insights

18. http://www.virgin.com/entrepreneur/richard-bransons-top-20-virgin-inspirational-insights

19. http://www.virgin.com/entrepreneur/richard-bransons-top-20-virgin-inspirational-insights

20. http://www.virgin.com/entrepreneur/richard-bransons-top-20-virgin-inspirational-insights

21. http://www.virgin.com/entrepreneur/richard-bransons-top-20-virgin-inspirational-insights

22. http://www.virgin.com/entrepreneur/richard-bransons-top-20-virgin-inspirational-insights

23. http://www.virgin.com/entrepreneur/richard-bransons-top-20-virgin-inspirational-insights

24. http://www.virgin.com/entrepreneur/richard-bransons-top-20-virgin-inspirational-insights

25. http://www.virgin.com/entrepreneur/richard-bransons-top-20-virgin-inspirational-insights

26. http://www.virgin.com/entrepreneur/richard-bransons-top-20-virgin-inspirational-insights

27. http://www.virgin.com/entrepreneur/richard-bransons-top-20-virgin-inspirational-insights

28. http://www.virgin.com/entrepreneur/richard-bransons-top-20-virgin-inspirational-insights

29. http://www.entrepreneur.com/article/249616

30. http://www.entrepreneur.com/article/249616

31. http://www.entrepreneur.com/article/249616

32. http://www.entrepreneur.com/article/249616
33. http://www.entrepreneur.com/article/249616
34. http://www.entrepreneur.com/article/249616
35. http://www.entrepreneur.com/article/249616
36. http://www.entrepreneur.com/article/249616
37. http://www.entrepreneur.com/article/249616
38. http://www.entrepreneur.com/article/249616
39. http://www.entrepreneur.com/article/249616
40. http://biz30.timedoctor.com/richard-bransons-six-secrets-to-productivity/
41. http://biz30.timedoctor.com/richard-bransons-six-secrets-to-productivity/
42. http://www.entrepreneur.com/article/217309
43. http://www.entrepreneur.com/article/217309
44. http://www.reuters.com/article/2015/06/23/us-virgin-cruise-line-idUSKBN0P326G20150623
45. http://www.reuters.com/article/2015/06/23/us-virgin-cruise-line-idUSKBN0P326G20150623
46. http://www.entrepreneur.com/article/217309
47. http://www.entrepreneur.com/article/217309
48. http://www.entrepreneur.com/article/217309
49. http://www.entrepreneur.com/article/217309
50. http://www.entrepreneur.com/article/217309
51. http://www.entrepreneur.com/article/217309
52. http://www.bbc.com/news/business-33281468
53. http://www.bbc.com/news/business-33281468
54. http://www.bbc.com/news/business-33281468
55. http://reneweconomy.com.au/2015/formula-e-can-overtake-formula-1-says-richard-branson-23114:
56. http://reneweconomy.com.au/2015/formula-e-can-overtake-formula-1-says-richard-branson-23114
57. http://reneweconomy.com.au/2015/formula-e-can-overtake-formula-1-says-richard-branson-23114
58. http://reneweconomy.com.au/2015/formula-e-can-overtake-formula-1-says-richard-branson-23114

59. http://www.afr.com/brand/chanticleer/virgins-richard-branson-pitches-nbn-alternative-to-malcolm-turnbull-20150908-gjhuag

60. http://www.afr.com/brand/chanticleer/virgins-richard-branson-pitches-nbn-alternative-to-malcolm-turnbull-20150908-gjhuag

61. http://www.afr.com/brand/chanticleer/virgins-richard-branson-pitches-nbn-alternative-to-malcolm-turnbull-20150908-gjhuag

62. http://www.afr.com/brand/chanticleer/virgins-richard-branson-pitches-nbn-alternative-to-malcolm-turnbull-20150908-gjhuag

63. http://www.afr.com/brand/chanticleer/virgins-richard-branson-pitches-nbn-alternative-to-malcolm-turnbull-20150908-gjhuag

64. http://www.traveller.com.au/virgin-galactic-longhaul-flight-plans-richard-branson-sees-australia-to-london-twohour-flights-gjmdui

65. http://www.traveller.com.au/virgin-galactic-longhaul-flight-plans-richard-branson-sees-australia-to-london-twohour-flights-gjmdui

66. http://www.ozarksfirst.com/news/richard-branson-eying-opportunities-in-branson

67. http://www.ozarksfirst.com/news/richard-branson-eying-opportunities-in-branson

68. http://learningenglish.voanews.com/content/vietnamese-businesses-learn-richard-branson/2963493.html

69. http://learningenglish.voanews.com/content/vietnamese-businesses-learn-richard-branson/2963493.html

70. http://learningenglish.voanews.com/content/vietnamese-businesses-learn-richard-branson/2963493.html

71. http://www.j4bgrants.co.uk/Default.aspx?WCI=htm Home&WCU=CBC=View,DSCODE=J4BGRB,NEWSI TEMID=38-N54081

Michael Joshua

ABOUT THE AUTHOR

Michael Joshua got his undergraduate degree in Finance and works full time at a large bank as a Financial Analyst. He has great knowledge in Business & Money, along with politics and technology.

Goodreads:
https://www.goodreads.com/user/show/46377085-michael-joshua

Twitter:
https://twitter.com/mjoshua_auth